Healthy, Happy, and Whole

Healthy, Happy, and Whole

Words of Encouragement from 20/20 Couples

(Twenty Couples who've been Married for 20 years or More!)

Dr. Thomas Adams

&

Lisa Sayles-Adams

ISBN 978-1-71688-574-7

Table of Contents

Acknowledgements

YOU COULD HAVE used your time to read any number of books out there, but you chose this one. We don't take that for granted. We poured a lot of ourselves into it this book and it was truly a labor of love.

We want to give a special thank you to Rob Joell for his input, framing, and constant reminder of who our audience is. A special thanks, also, to the many couples who contributed by sharing their words of wisdom; endured our pestering and trusted us with their stories.

Last, but certainly not least, we are thankful for each other. We have thought and talked long and hard about making this book a reality. We've been married over twenty-five years and our greatest joy, outside of each other and our children/grandchild, is mentoring other couples. That mentoring has brought us closer as a result.

Foreword

When two people marry, they leave their singular life behind and merge together with another person to become one. In fact, in the beginning, marriage can be described as a smooth and easy river, cool and calm with barely a ripple in the water. As the newness of marriage wares off, like a river, the once calm water can shift to rapid and moving waves that are not always contained in the river but can crash on the shores with a force of extreme weight and power as the river and the shore learn to interact as one. There are times when additional forces interact in a marriage and will bring storm like conditions causing unpredictable wind and rain making the river water overflow into other areas. This is when one must wait out the storm and trust the waters will recede back to their normal conditions.

As we talk to other married couples from the newly married to the seasoned senior or the second timer, we have learned no one walks into a marriage expecting anything less than a productive union. The path to a successful marriage is simple in theory but complex in the daily application of life. Two people from totally different backgrounds and many times conflicting views of life must learn to love, hope, forgive, build trust, commit, be kind, honor and cherish someone different than oneself. To apply the principles of marriage, one must sacrifice themselves for the love of another every day. Marriage is not passive but requires active engagement and participation from both parties to have a successful union.

Thomas and Lisa exemplify the foundation of marriage as they have navigated the waters and rivers of life. Their testimony is a clear example of 1 Corinthians 13:4-8, their Love is patient and kind. It does not envy or boast and is not proud. Their love does not dishonor others and is not self-seeking or easily angered. It does not delight in evil but rejoices with the truth. Their love always protects, always trusts, always hopes, always perseveres. Their love has never failed them.

Ministers Patrick and Stephanie Burrage, Ed. D (Author of Jewels for Every Woman: A Guide for *Queendom* Living)

Introduction

MARRIAGE. MARRIAGE. MARRIAGE. It seems like marriage has been a polarizing topic for decades. Why do people get married? Why do people stay married? Is marriage even worth it? Whether they think it's taken too casually or isn't receiving the respect it deserves, people always seem to have an opinion regarding matrimony and those who engage in it.

You might have heard, for example, that marriage in the African American community doesn't last. Fewer individuals are getting married all the time, people say, and even fewer keep their families together in a healthy atmosphere. It's become increasingly common that FOX, CNN, MSNBC, and many other news outlets post weekly opinions on the "breakdown of the African American family."

This is not the world in which we live. There are many long-lasting and positive African American marriages. President Barrack and Michelle Obama are probably the most famous example, at the moment, but they are far from the only example available.

My wife and I are writing this book as sort of a clarion call – to bring awareness to stories of incredibly committed and happy couples who have been married for decades. After years of being mentors to couples around the country, we decided to put something together that celebrates the beauty of African American marriage.

We interviewed over twenty couples to get their 'best practices' for keeping a loving relationship. These are couples from all walks of life. Highly educated PhDs, carpenters and electricians, teachers, police officers, warehouse managers, call center staff – just everyday people. We are thankful that they took the time to share their most precious gift with us – themselves.

Together, we'd like to share thoughts on what qualities contribute to a strong and healthy marriage. While the themes identified in this book are universal and can be applied to any marriage, we wanted to specifically lift-up African American marriages as they seem to have increasingly come under attack. This book is a true labor of love for us. We hope it will inspire hope in your life and help you build your own committed marriage, be it now or in the future.

Chapter 1: Love

LOVE IS A common word that is often thrown about with no real definition. We know that we "love" our partners, for example, but what exactly does that mean? What does it look like in practice and how is it expressed in successful marriages? These are all great questions. Let's look at the concept of love and how it can help you maintain and sustain a healthy marriage for the long haul.

What Does it Mean to "Love?"

As mentioned above, almost everyone will say they love their partner. Sometimes it's important to stop and take a second to really think about what that means – what emotions and effort go into the idea of love and how it is expressed in marriage. We think there are three main components to love that form healthy relationships:

1. Feeling

2. Action

3. Attachment

Love is a feeling, certainly, but you can also act in a loving manner towards your partner – it is an action as well as an emotion, in other words. Love is also an attachment to an individual that is strong and deep and lasts as the years pass. Each component is an important one to understand.

1. Love as a feeling. Love is a deep-seated emotion that is difficult to describe. It's a feeling that drives you to be with someone. When you find yourself thinking about your spouse long after you've said goodbye for the day and eagerly anticipate your next interaction, you're feeling love for them. It's a type of attraction that moves beyond the physical and transcends to something almost spiritual in nature. You are drawn to your spouse because you enjoy them as a person – you recognize their quirks and understand their beliefs and personality and enjoy being in their company.

Another aspect of love as a feeling is a sense of freedom and selflessness. When you love someone, you aren't jealous of their accomplishments. Instead, you celebrate their successes and talent because you feel proud of their achievements. When something good happens to them, you're grateful for it. In other situations, watching someone succeed and experience good things might create jealousy – but when it comes to someone you love, you enjoy their successes and good fortune as much as you would your own. And, of course, to a certain extent, they are. Spouses share hardships and victories alike; they multiply each other's joys and ease each other's sorrows.

In addition to everything we've described above, love also has the power to help see you through difficult times. It is an empowering feeling at its core, and grants you trust and affection to your spouse.

2. Love as an Action. We know that love can be a feeling, but it is equally an action. Life can be incredibly difficult, and it is inevitable that you and your spouse will face hardships, particularly if you're together for the span of a lifetime. The exact situations in question don't matter nearly as much as how you face them. Here, too, love can help.

When you behave in a loving manner, you are putting the well-being and happiness of your partner first. That might seem like an obvious and straightforward thing to do in a marriage, but you might be surprised at just how hard it can be when you're exhausted and stressed from work and childcare. All you might want to do is grasp any measure of "alone time" in which to care for yourself – but instead, despite being overwhelmed, you make your partner and their needs a priority. This is love, and it is something that both partners should strive to achieve.

Love isn't a single action – it is the result of many choices you make throughout your relationship. These are deliberate choices that are made on a daily basis. It is something you should be conscious of and actively attempt to show your partner. Don't rely on them to know you love them – *show* them that you love them. Love is an action. Let hardship draw you closer together instead of pushing you apart, make their needs a priority, and have faith that they will do the same for you.

3. Love as Attachment. Finally, love is something that deepens from excitement and attraction to attachment. Many relationships start off with strong emotions, but few of them deepen into a true attachment to your partner. This is the aspect of love that ensures you and your partner are dedicated to each other and will fight for your relationship. It's something that begins once you're through the heady "puppy love" stage and will last throughout the rest of your lives together.

Attachment is perhaps one of the most important and satisfying aspects of love. More than anything else, it brings you and your spouse closer together and keeps the motivation to make the relationship work as high as possible. This is what helps create those long-term relationships that are based in respect and affection. Do not overlook this part of love. Know that your actions can help foster this attachment.

A Note About Communication

This is something we'll take a closer look at a bit later in the book, but we believe communication is an incredibly important part of love. Maintaining open lines of communication with your spouse will help you each understand where the other is coming from.

Promoting this kind of understanding is invaluable in any relationship, but especially when it comes to marriage. You must make the effort to communicate with your partner, yes, but equally important is the process of *listening* to what they're telling you. Love means caring about your partner's feelings and working to understand why they feel the way they do. What is important to them, and why do they feel that way? Being able to answer these questions is a sign of a close and healthy relationship but *wanting* to answer them – to figure out what makes your partner tick – is an important part of love.

When we come right down to it, *love* is the term we use to describe the feeling of respect, adoration, and affection we have for our spouses. It's a term that indicates we want to grow with them and create a life together. There are a lot of ideas about what love is supposed to look like, but the fact of the matter is that there is no right or wrong way to love in a healthy, committed relationship. In fact, there are a variety of ways to express love for your partner.

What Does Love Look Like in a Committed and Long-Term Marriage?

We've talked about the different aspects of love and the importance of each, but what does it look like in a committed marriage? A few of the couples we've interviewed will help answer that question.

Robert and Sharon. Robert Reese and Sharon have been married for 24 years. They discussed a few different guidelines that have helped them maintain their marriage. One of the most important was maintaining faith and love in each other, which helps them to "One, weather the difficult times; two, respect the changes and growth that will occur in both of us and remind us that our love is rooted in so much more than our physical attributes."

We talked about this earlier, but love is much more than physical attraction. It's a much deeper connection that can sustain you through times both good and bad.

Stephanie and Patrick. Married for 27 years, Stephanie and Patrick concur that maintaining a relationship of love and respect is incredibly important in their marriage. They say they "try to fight fairly and we never go to bed angry. We resolve issues before nightfall. Your spouse should be your best friend. We date weekly and enjoy each other's company. We put God first, our relationship second, with children/family next." Maintaining a relationship based in love and understanding requires effort, and they recommend focusing on it as much as possible.

Roy and Shonda. Roy and Shonda, married 22 years, have a lot to say about love! They believe that hard work sustains love and can sustain your marriage, too. The following is what they shared with us:

"What I have come to understand about marriage is that, in order to preserve it and keep it healthy, it will require work! I love my wife with everything in me. I have learned that love demands our best effort; just uttering the words isn't enough. Wrapped up in that four-letter word is sacrifice, selflessness, compromise, disappointment, forgiveness, and hope. A simple formula that I apply to my marriage is prefer one another, if we practice that we will seldom let each other down."

Angela and Duschene. Finally, Angela and Duschene, married 22 years, believe that love is absolutely vital to their relationship. This is what they had to say when asked about how they had maintained a healthy and strong marriage for over two decades:

"We're best friends. We're partners. We're lovers. We're confidants.

"We believe in each other and we believe in us. We're each other's sounding boards, sharing our hopes, dreams, and fears. We love each other, flaws and all. That means we root for each other. We play together. We listen to each other. We're vulnerable with each other. We're honest with each other. And we're nice to each other.

"Every day, we walk and build the bridge that will carry us through the rest of our lives. We may not always know where we're going but we know we're going there together. We're in this for the long haul. Believing that is key to getting over the bumps (and seeing them as merely bumps) and the key to really appreciating the best days (and magnifying our joy). The highs, lows and everything in between are all part of the story we're writing together."

In closing, love is a complicated word that plays an important role in healthy marriages. It's not easy to define nor is it easy to maintain, but it is something that offers a payoff that is much greater than the amount of effort put into it.

Chapter 2: Loyalty

THERE ARE MANY factors that go into building and maintaining a healthy marriage, but few are as important as loyalty. Any long-term relationship takes work and isn't always easy to maintain. That's especially true in a marriage, where sorrows and joys are shared in equal measure and life, sometimes, seems to conspire against health and happiness.

This difficulty is perhaps one of the reasons why loyalty is so important. Your relationship should be a sanctuary in which you can rest assured that your partner has your best interests in mind. Instead of contributing to the stresses of everyday life, marriage should ultimately be a relationship that makes everyone involved stronger than they are on their own.

Much like love, loyalty is a term that is often repeated without much thought. People are all too quick to state its importance without ever really giving the reality and definition of the word any consideration. Before we can talk about what loyalty looks like in a committed and long-term marriage, then, we must, first, understand what the word means.

What Does it Mean to be "Loyal?"

The belief that loyalty is vital in a long-term and committed relationship is nearly universal. Less common, however, is knowledge of the word's definition. Outside of specifically love relationships, the word imparts a sense of obligation. It calls to mind the importance of being faithful to your obligations, to your word, and to your engagements.

When the word is used in reference to marriage and committed relationships, its definition differs slightly. It becomes less a matter of obligation and more one of dedication and devotion that is freely given. It is an important part of love, in fact, and is one of the word's defining characteristics. Note that more than physical fidelity, loyalty also implies emotional commitment and devotion.

There are a variety of different ways that loyalty can be expressed in a committed and long-term relationship. If you are loyal to your partner, you are respectful of their weaknesses and their strengths. You act in such a way that helps strengthen them without judgement or shame. You don't seek to embarrass or shame your partner, especially not in public. Part of loyalty is maintaining and presenting a united front to the world and to your family. Conflict and discord disrupt that front.

A loyal partner gives their spouse their attention and time and assures them that this will always be the case. A loyal partner is a partner who is available to listen to their spouse when they experience difficulties and is there to help as much as possible. Because it is born of trust, loyalty also means keeping confidences and refraining from telling other people about your spouse's weaknesses or fears.

Being loyal to your partner means giving their needs, their concerns, and their opinions attention and weight. On a more practical level, it means thinking about how your words and actions might impact them before you make a decision. Loyalty is not something that is easy to practice. This is especially true when it comes to a long-term relationship.

Marriage, in particular, is a relationship that is full of give and take – one that thrives on trust, love, and compromise. In times of hardship . . . and there will be more than a few . . . disloyalty is often seen as the easier path to take. It takes less effort to care about your own interests first and send your partner's interests to the back of your mind than it does to consider their feelings, especially when the relationship is out of the "honeymoon" phase.

Choose the path less often walked and pick loyalty above convenience. This is how you build a truly healthy and happy marriage that can weather almost any storm it faces.

What Does Loyalty Look Like in a Committed and Long-Term Marriage?

Even more than love, loyalty is a difficult term to define. Instead of dedicating hundreds of pages discussing its intricacies and its importance, we think giving you practical examples and advice is the best option. Many of the couples we interviewed talked about just how important loyalty and commitment are in building and sustaining a long-term and successful marriage.

Milton and Kendra. Milton and Kendra, a couple married for 17 years, were kind enough to give us detailed advice pertaining to maintaining a happy marriage. At the forefront of their thoughts is the importance of loyalty and commitment. In fact, they believe that "Marriage is more commitment than love. Love can be fleeting, but the commitment to stay and grow together is lasting." The conscious decision to remain together, despite the hardships life presents, is often the most important aspect of an enduring marriage. Having loyalty to each other and to a shared vision of a long-term marriage, in other words, is critical to a successful marriage. The same couple continues:

"We've been married 17 years and have three kids. We last because we respect what our commitment is to each other and to the God we serve . . . You fight through the ups and downs of a loved one's career, life challenges, and, sometimes, health. None of which are forecasted, and this is where commitment manifests itself."

Now, we don't mean to make marriage sound as though it is a chore rather than a path of joy. The fact of the matter, however, is that a long-term marriage simply isn't easy to maintain. Think about the first 20 years of your life and how much you grew and changed during that time. Think about how life's difficulties popped up, unexpectedly, and took an immense amount of courage to overcome.

Marriage will also experience these ups and downs. It is not a failing on the couple in question, but rather a fact of life. Understanding and accepting this is vital to creating a strong, long-term marriage – one that can last through changing circumstances. Loyalty is what will keep you both together even when everything else in life seems to be falling apart.

Tonya and Phillip. Tonya and Philip, a couple married for 23 years, also credits loyalty and commitment with the success of their marriage. They understand that making the decision to commit to each other and to become one in mind and action is vital. "Marriage is about unity," they say, "and being joined as one, remembering why you decided to exchange vows and remaining committed to your words and each other . . . sometimes it's easier to get out than stay in, and you have to want it." Marriage is a lifetime commitment and can span decades, but it's not an easy decision nor is it something to take lightly.

When we talk about "unity" and the importance of remaining committed to each other, what we're really talking about is loyalty. The decision to maintain your relationship through thick and the thin – to love and cherish each other even when it isn't easy – is essentially loyalty incarnate. If you're serious about remaining together and building a long-term, strong marriage, then you have to make the decision to be loyal to each other, even when life is difficult.

Kevin and Felicia. Yet another couple who emphasizes the importance of loyalty in their marriage is Kevin and Felicia, who have been married for 19 years. Their take on the subject focuses on the importance of building a strong unit and ensuring that you continue to nurture it throughout the years.

"No matter how low you fall or how high you climb, always, always, always ensure that your marriage and family are a source of joy and love in your life. Putting this first ensures you don't get lost in work, play or anywhere else you may find yourself spending time."

This advice is important because, in addition to underlining how important it is to create a strong relationship based in trust and loyalty, it also emphasizes the joy and love that a marriage has to offer. Sometimes it's easy to forget to simply enjoy your spouse and your family. Revel in your marriage and appreciate the relationship you have built and maintained with your partner. Instead of looking outside your marriage for joy or distraction, you should look inside it for motivation and love. Marriage can be difficult at times, yes, but the rewards for the effort you expend are incredible.

Never forget just how important your relationship and your marriage are to your life and treat them as such.

Larry and Pam. Married 25 years, Larry and Pam had a wealth of advice to share with us. One of the things they emphasized was, again, loyalty and commitment to each other.

"After 25 years of marriage we have grown to appreciate: Never keep secrets. Trust is key to our success . . . The couple relationship takes priority (even when children are involved). Never let other family members and/or friends come between you. It's important to always see ourselves as a team. Together we can conquer any challenge. After 25 years of marriage there have been many."

We love this advice because it's relevant and so important to a successful marriage. Don't let other people interfere with your marriage! Your loyalty is to yourself and your spouse. We talked about this a little bit earlier in the chapter, too. You shouldn't seek to discuss the intimate details of your marriage, or your spouse, with people outside your marriage. Don't bring additional people into your relationship – you'll have enough work on your hands just trying to handle the two of you! Remember that you are building a loyal and united relationship, not one that cracks any time a friend or family member tries to involve themselves in your business. Larry and Pam also had this to say:

"No marriage is perfect! We are not trying to live up to a fairy tale. We have the ability to make our relationship what we want it to be. It will not be perfect, and others may not understand why we do what we do. That's okay, as long as we are happy, and it works for us. Marriage is not about pleasing anyone but your partner."

This is perhaps one of the best examples of loyalty we could have included here. Marriage is not about achieving perfection nor is it about meeting someone else's idea of "right." Your loyalty is to your spouse and your marriage and, to that end, it's important to do what works for you both.

To summarize, loyalty is the act of remaining true to your spouse in word and emotion. It is born of love and devotion, not obligation, and is one of the single most important aspects of any marriage.

Chapter 3: Communication

SUCCESSFUL LONG-TERM marriages are marriages in which spouses stay in a constant state of learning. They learn about each other, they learn about how to function in society, and they learn how to grow together, as a team. This is vital to the success of a marriages that will last and really go the distance.

While there are a variety of factors that contribute towards this state of learning and loving, communication is likely one of the most important. It is through communication, for example, that spouses learn about each other. Although they typically cannot be together every second of the day, they are each able to be involved in the other's life by frequent and honest conversation, for example.

More than keeping spouses abreast of changes in their separate personal lives, however, communication ensures that spouses understand how the other is feeling and what they think about various things. It helps identify any potential issues before they become marriage-ending problems, too, and allows spouses to at least attempt to grow together. Without communication, people quickly grow apart, and serious issues begin arising.

We want to ensure that you truly understand how to keep communication going in your relationship and how it can help you build a strong relationship that can endure the worst of life's surprises.

How Do you Maintain Healthy Communication in a Marriage?

Before we get started talking about what healthy communication looks like in a relationship, let's talk about how you can keep these important lines open throughout the years. It is not unusual for open communication to wane as time passes, so make sure that you keep these tips in mind as your relationship grows. Knowing the risks and taking steps to prevent them is half the battle.

Talk openly to each other. First of all, you have to be open about any issues that arise in your relationship. That means that you should be able to speak with your spouse with the utmost honesty. You want a relationship that can withstand challenges as well as triumphs, but that kind of strength doesn't develop without serious effort. Open communication is a vital part of building the kind of marriage that withstands even the longest and leanest of years.

Make speaking openly with your partner a priority in your relationship. That means that you take time, on a regular basis, to sit down and discuss anything that is on your mind, including things that have been bothering you in your relationship (or even just in your everyday life). Doing this helps ensure that any issues that might arise between you and your partner are resolved quickly and easily before they become significant issues.

Life can be busy, so it's a good idea to schedule this kind of talk in advance. You don't have to write down specific topics to discuss (although you certainly can if the mood strikes you) but setting aside time designed specifically to sit and talk with your spouse will help strengthen your relationship more than you can imagine.

Be supportive. Support your partner in all they do and expect the same support from them in turn. Doing this helps reinforce the idea that you're in this relationship for the long haul and are willing to grow with your partner as the years pass. This includes being respectful about your spouse's job, their strengths, and their weaknesses. Don't belittle them or dismiss their accomplishments or frustrations.

Even if it's difficult for you to truly understand where your partner is coming from sometimes, do your very best to be positive for them regardless. If you encounter an issue that you're really struggling to be supportive about, refer to the tip directly above this one and be honest about it. Discussing these concerns openly can help you learn about your partner and how they think.

Listen first. We've been talking about how important it is to talk to each other, and it's true – you have to effectively communicate with your partner. With that said, it is equally important to be able to sit down, put your concerns aside, and listen to your partner as they're speaking. That doesn't mean tuning them out and just agreeing or saying what you think they want to hear. Truly listening to your spouse means giving them your undivided attention and doing your best to understand what they're saying, why they're saying it, and how you can best support them.

Note that this doesn't mean you never get to voice your own concerns. Listening is a two-way street. You should receive just as much as you are giving, and it's okay to expect your partner to be willing to listen to what you have to say, too. Be courteous and respectful of each other, but don't shove your own needs aside indefinitely to take care of someone else's needs.

Break down those walls. It can be so easy to put up guards designed to keep yourself from getting hurt. This is especially true when we get into arguments or disagreements with our loved ones.

It's normal to not want to be hurt. It's equally normal to experience an event in which our feelings were bruised and want to avoid that kind of situation in the future. That's where those barriers come from. They spring from the desire to avoid being hurt, and they can quickly grow to create a veritable moat around your emotions and your life that only serves to keep your spouse firmly out.

Don't put up walls! Refer to the previous tips. Communicate about your feelings and why you're hurting. Talk to your spouse about how to avoid repeating this situation in the future. Learn from these situations and move on – don't allow them to pull your relationship apart.

Stay positive. Communication isn't always easy. In fact, it can sometimes be discouraging and uncomfortable and can tempt you into frustration with yourself and your partner. Before you give in to that temptation, however, take a step back and just breathe for a few minutes. Getting upset and negative with your partner (or even just about your partner) accomplishes nothing good. All it will do is push you both farther apart and encourage those troublesome walls from above to spring up unheeded.

Instead of becoming frustrated, do your very best to stay positive. There is something positive to take away from every conversation, even if that is just being grateful that the topic is out in the open and now you can work on addressing it so it's never an issue again. Approach interactions in a positive manner and devote yourself to facilitating productive communication with your spouse.

It's okay to be emotional. There is a difference between being emotionally open with your partner and being too emotional to listen. It is good to freely share your emotions with your partner. You want to be able to understand where they are coming from, after all, and to help them understand where you are coming from as well. Be open enough to share your feelings, but make sure you're calm enough to listen as well as speak.

Maintain the trust. We've talked about how important trust is in any relationship. It's no different when we're talking about communication. Make sure you are speaking with your partner honestly and respectfully – make it easy for them to trust that you have their best intentions in mind. At the same time, you have to be able to trust in your partner without reservations. This unconditional trust, fostered by consistent, healthy communication, will help you build a relationship that will truly last the ages.

What Does Healthy Communication Look Like in a Committed Long-Term Marriage?

As you can see from above, healthy communication is absolutely vital in a long-term marriage. Aside from paying heed to the tips presented above, what does maintaining honest and open communication with your spouse mean when you've been married for decades? To help answer this question, let's see what the couples we interviewed have to say on the subject.

Thomas and Lisa. Marriage is all about having those intimate discussions as often as possible. It is important to note, however, that you have to keep those discussions to yourself rather than telling other people all about them. As Thomas and Lisa, married for 25 years, put it, "Marriage is a way of life, not an event. Keep people out of your bedroom - figuratively and literally. You can't strengthen your marriage by inviting everyone with an opinion into your intimate discussions and deliberations." You should be able to communicate openly and honestly with your partner without worrying about someone else finding out about your concerns and fears.

Keep other people out of your marriage and keep that important communication between you and your spouse.

Steven and Leadriane. No matter how much we say it, it's impossible to overstate the importance of communication in a healthy and long-term relationship. Steven and Leadriane, married 31 years, put it quite simply by advising that everyone "Keep lines of communication open and keep other people out of your marriage." This is a simple guideline to keep in mind, and a recurring one that was present amongst the majority of our couples.

Keep communicating with each other and keep that communication open between you and your spouse. In other words, rely on each other for support and help, not everyone else you know. Keep each other's trust and only bring outside help in if that's something you've both agreed to do.

Gary and Tina. In large part, this chapter has been dedicated to discussing the kind of communication that you should have with your spouse. That communication is honest and open in nature and can really help to keep your marriage going even when you're exhausted and ready to give up. Gary and Tina, married for 23 years, advise, "Listen to each other and remember you're on the same team! Be honest, flexible, and open to change." Above all, you must listen when you communicate. Speaking without listening is a surefire way to ensure potentially serious issues and concerns are never addressed and, before you realize what is happening, they blow up into something big.

Be honest and open when you communicate with each other. This is important! Don't just say something you think your partner would like to hear. Keep your conversation flexible and listen to what your partner is telling you.

Alexander and Lisa. Finally, let's look at what Alexander and Lisa, married for 20 years, have to say about marriage and communication. "Communication is more than idle conversation," they say. "Having hard discussions with your partner without being judgmental [is important]." We think this particular advice is fantastic because it doesn't shy away from the idea that not all communication is easy. We talked about this briefly above, but it bears repeating: Communication can be difficult!

Communication can lead to a lot of soul-searching and worried moments. That doesn't mean that it's something you should avoid, however, because that soul-searching and concern helps lead to a strengthened relationship. Instead, embrace even the most difficult of topics and ensure that your spouse understands you will always be there for them – they need to know that, no matter the topic in question, you're ready to listen to what they have to say.

Communication is a vital component of a successful and healthy relationship. This is especially true of long-term marriages and is important in keeping the lines of communication open and honest. Failing to do this will quickly lead to serious issues in your marriage – issues that could have been avoided if you had only been able to talk to each other before they became seemingly insurmountable. For the health of your marriage, make communicating with your spouse a priority.

Chapter 4: Child Rearing & Discipline

WE ALREADY KNOW that marriage is hard work, right? It demands a lot of time and attention, not to mention communication and dedication, to truly last. It's important to talk to your spouse before making decisions that impact you both, and it's important to keep other people out of your marriage. But, while these are vital guidelines to keep in mind on a daily basis, they are, perhaps, even more pertinent when children are involved.

Raising children is something that is difficult, at times, even for the best of parents and most obedient and good-natured of children. It's just about impossible to raise another human being without encountering at least a few challenging moments. The way you raise your child is vitally important to their overall success, both today and in the future. That means that it is important to make sure that you have a clear idea of the kind of values you and your spouse are working to instill in them.

Do not make the mistake of attempting to take on the burden and stresses of child rearing all on your own! As with anything else in life, you and your spouse are partners. As a team, then, you should work to raise your children. That means you share everything – the happy times as well as the trying ones. Let's take a closer look at exactly how you can work with your spouse to raise and discipline your children in a marriage.

How Do you Work Together to Raise and Discipline Children in a Marriage?

There is an odd thing that tends to happen far too often in a marriage once children are involved. One parent tends to become the "main parent." They handle the majority of the child rearing responsibilities, including assessing and handing down discipline, as well as the more mundane, everyday activities like helping a child with their homework or answering their questions and concerns. This is *not* how you work together to raise children in a marriage. That's not to say that some children won't feel closer to one parent than the other at some point and seek out their counsel, but both parents should make themselves available to their children as well as their spouse on a daily basis.

When you have children in a marriage, the need to work together and present a unified front is more important than ever. This can be difficult, especially if you have different views on parenting and the way to go about raising children. That's one of the reasons it's important to speak with your spouse about these issues. The first step in working together to raise healthy, happy children, then, is communication with your spouse. This shouldn't come as a surprise at this point – communication is one of the most important factors in a successful marriage in general. It makes sense that it is important when something as delicate and potentially dividing as children are involved.

Speak with your spouse and have frank conversations about how you see yourself raising your children. This is something that can be done well in advance of the arrival of said children. In fact, it is probably best that you broach this topic before any children are in the picture. Doing so gives you time to examine where you and your partner each stand in your individual parenting styles and beliefs. You might be surprised to find out that you have different ideas about how things like discipline should be administered, or what kinds of actions deserve discipline in the first place. Discovering these opposing viewpoints is an important step in the parenting process and shouldn't necessarily be seen as a bad thing.

If you find that you and your spouse don't agree about certain aspects of parenting, I'd ask you to go back through the previous chapters in this book for information on how to proceed. Staying calm and showing respect to each other, while honestly discussing your feelings and beliefs, will be vitally important to overcoming these issues. Seeking out the counsel of a couple you trust and admire, or from your church elders, might also prove to be incredibly helpful.

Keep in mind that the end result of these conversations is both of you arriving to the same conclusion about how you will parent your children. That might mean that both of you will bend your own personal beliefs a bit to meet the other in the middle, and that's okay. It's also okay if this process is one that takes a while. As long as you keep the lines of communication open and treat each other with love and respect, you will eventually come to understand the other's view and determine a parenting style to which you can both dedicate yourselves.

As an aside, don't be afraid to throw in extreme hypotheticals when talking to your spouse. Ask them how they think you, as a couple and parents, should respond if the worst-case scenario – whatever that might be in your mind – should happen with your child. What kind of discipline will you administer and how will you go about doing that? Work together to create a parenting plan so that you can work together to parent in harmony, with both of you maintaining important roles in your child's life.

What Does Healthy Child Rearing and Discipline Look like in a Committed and Long-Term Marriage?

Child rearing and discipline, as described above, are both issues you should discuss with your spouse. This will help you understand how to proceed with your children and how to remain united even in the face of extreme stress. Ideally, discipline and child rearing will be a smooth process where both parents are on the same page about the decisions to be made.

Note that, while parenting is important and will undoubtedly take up quite a bit of your time and energy, it should not signal an end to your personal relationship with your spouse. It is important to make maintaining and strengthening your marriage a priority. Take some time every day to talk to each other about things other than your children. Take date nights as regularly as you can, and consciously work on remaining close and happy with your partner. This is what a healthy marriage looks like when children are involved. That's not to say that there might not be moments when parenting takes priority and a date night will be canceled as a result, but this should be something that happens infrequently and not as a standard occurrence.

It's okay to have a set night every week (or every month – whatever works for your schedule) that everyone in the household knows is reserved for you and your spouse. In fact, it's a great idea! This is especially true once your children are old enough to take care of themselves and each other for short periods of time. You don't have to dedicate every single moment of your day to parenting, and you shouldn't feel guilty about taking an evening "off" to enjoy the company of your spouse.

Finally, keep in mind that the advice given in earlier chapters about keeping other people out of your marriage also applies when it comes to the topic of parenting. You might be surprised at how much advice you receive after you have children. While some of it will be incredibly valuable, much of it will be unwarranted and come with an unwanted critique of your parenting style. Keep in mind that your partner is the only person you really need to answer to, and if you're on the same page about how your children should be parented, then others' opinions shouldn't really matter. Make decisions with your spouse, not with random individuals offering their own beliefs. The exception, of course, is when you and your spouse make the decision to seek counsel about a particular issue or situation. That advice is absolutely something you should discuss together and implement as you deem it appropriate.

Child Rearing and Discipline in Healthy Marriages

Our couples have some thoughts about this topic.

Alan and Mickey. The first comes from Alan and Mickey, who have been married for 26 years. When it comes to keeping their marriage strong, they had this to say:

"One thing we agreed upon beforehand was, when we get married, there won't be a divorce! So, there have been major ups and downs, but we've stood on what we said from the beginning. We also believe in home cooked meals and our kids' education and trying not to step on each other's toes when it comes to our children and/or grandchildren. The main and most important thing to longevity in our marriage is to keep extended family and outsiders out of our in-house business!"

This is great advice that we think should be heeded. Respect each other when it comes to your children. Discuss big decisions before making them, and don't contradict each other or interrupt each other's plans. Address issues as they arise and avoid allowing them time to fester and create rifts that are difficult to heal.

Stephanie and Pat. Stephanie and Pat, who have been married for 27 years, had this to say about how they've kept their relationship strong:

"We try to fight fairly, and we never go to bed angry. We resolve issues before nightfall. Your spouse should be your best friend. We date weekly and enjoy each other's company. We put God first, our relationship second, with children/family next."

This is important advice and it harkens back to what we said about making your relationship a priority even after children are involved. Your relationship must be something that you take just as seriously as you take raising your children. Dedicate time and effort toward maintaining a healthy relationship.

Larry and Pam. Married for 25 years, Larry and Pam also shared their insight into maintaining a healthy relationship. They shared that, "After 25 years of marriage we have grown to appreciate that it's important to have positive older couples in your life. People you admire and who can serve as a role model."

This is something we briefly touched upon earlier. When you meet a couple with the kind of marriage you want to have, it's okay to try to emulate, in your own marriage, the things they do well in their marriage. This can include parenting style. Don't be afraid to reach out for advice from a more experienced couple should the need arise – everyone needs an outside perspective at some point in time. Just make sure it's a decision that you and your spouse make together.

Larry and Pam also shared that "The couple identity is important, and each person has a role and responsibility to do their part to support the relationship to grow and thrive . . . the couple relationship takes priority (even when children are involved)."

Your identity as a couple is vitally important to building and maintaining a strong relationship with your spouse. That's one of the reasons why it's so important to make time for your relationship as something separate from parenting. This is advice that has been echoed by more than a few couples at this point, and it has helped many marriages thrive and grow even stronger after children arrived.

When it comes to parenting and child rearing, it is possible to make the experience easier by discussing your goals and beliefs with your spouse as honestly and early as possible. Pay attention to disagreements and respectfully work your way through them (and seek counsel if you both decide, as a couple, that you need an outside perspective). Don't overrule or contradict each other and do your best to always remember that you are a team. That includes taking time out to care for each other and your personal relationship whenever possible and doing so consistently and without guilt. The stronger your marriage is, the easier it will be to raise healthy and well-adjusted children. Finally, keep the lines of communication open at all times, and always treat each other with respect.

Chapter 5: Financial Literacy

UP TO THIS point, we've been focusing on issues that are largely related to communication and loyalty. We've discussed these topics in detail and have examined how to effectively love your spouse, respect your spouse, communicate with your spouse in various situations in life. In this chapter, we're going to look at something that might seem as though it doesn't fit the mold we've been building. Finances, although a bit less spiritual and a bit more material, is a topic that you and your spouse must master in order to build a healthy and lasting marriage – and you might find that it takes every skill we've been discussing in this book to do so.

In this chapter, we're going to look at money and financial literacy. As the old saying goes, money makes the world go 'round! On an everyday basis, it is important to have a solid understanding about how you're making money, where you're spending it, what you should be saving for, and how you can make the best possible financial decisions. Whether or not we agree with the way obtaining money has become a seemingly endless quest in life, it is important that we understand the basics of it in order to succeed as both as individuals and as a family unit.

What does money have to do with marriage? Some people will wonder why we're bothering with this topic, while others will immediately understand its importance. Dr. Melanie Joell, a family therapist in Maryland, states that arguments about or over money are some of, if not the single greatest contributors, to broken marriages. If we have enough money, we will be able to more easily take care of ourselves and our children even in worst-case scenarios.

On the other hand, if we don't have enough money, life can become an almost unbearable grind that can stress even the most even-tempered person. Just as important as having money, or not having money (whichever the case might be), of course, is what we do with it and how we spend it. Those decisions create stress that weighs on marriages, too.

Let's talk about money, financial literacy, and how you and your spouse can work together to not only exercise good financial decisions, but to help make your marriage stronger in the process.

What Does it Mean to be "Financially Literate?"

Financial literacy is a term that references an individual's ability to understand money, including things like budgeting, in order to make good financial decisions. With that understanding, the term is a bit more complex than it may appear. Think about the term "literacy" for a moment. In order to be considered literate, you must have the ability to read and *comprehend* the words you take in. For example, recognizing that a particular combination of letters equals something called a "word" without any understanding regarding what that word actually means, is not the same thing as being literate. In other words, you may know that the letters C-A-T spell cat – but if you don't know what a cat is, you're reading but not comprehending. That's why, in books for beginning readers, there is a picture next to the word being taught. Literacy refers to a more nuanced or complex understanding of reading comprehension.

Financial literacy, then, is a term that also demands a more complex understanding of money and how it works. This is something beyond "I work to earn money and use money to buy things." You can think of financial literacy as the combination of skills, knowledge, and confidence needed to make responsible, smart financial decisions. This is a skill that not everyone possesses, and if not developed, it can create a significant amount of stress in your everyday life, as well as your marriage. Financial literacy is a complex understanding of money and it is often influenced by life experiences, philosophy, and training. You and your spouse will clearly have different life experiences and will more than likely have different philosophies and training. As we've written repeatedly, communication with one another is the key to understanding your differences so that you can complement one another in building a financially literate household.

Debt management. One of the most important reasons to ensure you and your spouse are financially savvy is to ensure that you manage debt effectively. In the United States, more individuals and households are in debt than ever before. Debt, especially when it accumulates, can be a financial cancer. When large amounts of debt are incurred without income to balance it out, the debt lowers your credit score, reduces your chances of getting loans or credit cards, and/or increases the interest rate (the charge for borrowing money) on loans you receive. Being concerned about large amounts of debt can cause emotional, psychological, and physical stress that can attack a family. Debt management is a technique used to assess the kind of debt you have, determine how to effectively budget around that debt depending upon the income that you have, and how to repay the debt as quickly as possible.

Budgeting. Financially literate households have a solid handle on both the importance of budgeting and the best ways to plan an effective budget. This will provide for the family's needs and allow for smoother household operation so you don't find yourself in the habit of saying, "Wait until payday." One simple way to create a budget for your household is to JOINTLY place the amounts of all bills and expenses on a piece of paper or electronic spreadsheet if you are comfortable with a computer. Make sure to include an amount for unexpected expenses because we all have an them pop up during the month.

Next, create a list of all the money/revenue that comes into the house. If your expenses exceed your revenue, you have some choices to make. Namely, you can reduce expenses, bring in more revenue, or opt for a combination of both. Financially illiterate people "buy their wants and beg their needs." That means that you impulsively buy a luxury item (car, clothing, concert tickets) but then have to ask for help to pay for a necessity (day care, rent/mortgage, utilities, etc.). Remember, you don't have to buy everything you want. You now have a visual that you and your spouse can use to help manage your monthly financial operations. Discipline yourselves to follow it!

Effective saving. When you're financially literate it means you probably know and are aware of the best ways to save money. When saving, you should consider short and long-term goals. Oftentimes, there are small things one can do to save money (i.e., unplug coffee machines and other small electronic appliances, lower your heat and increase the temperature of the air conditioner, or choose to cook instead of going out. There are many books and resources available to help you find tips for saving money. Creating a budget and sticking to it is all about planning and discipline. Financially literate individuals have a good grasp on both the importance of and the best ways to create an effective budget that allows for a family's needs but not necessarily all of their wants.

You pay other people every month (car, mortgage, utilities, entertainment, etc.) – now, you must discipline yourself to pay yourself every month, as well. Start with saving one to three percent of your income with the goal of saving up three to six months of cash reserve. This means that if there is a financial hardship you encountered (loss of job, loss of vehicle, etc.) you would have the means to continue paying for necessities for a period of time. The ability to consider long-term goals, like buying a house or paying for your child's college education, while creating a budget that allows you to save and grow money over time is one that will serve both you and your family well.

What Does Financial Literacy Look Like in a Committed and Long-Term Marriage?

Marriage is a huge decision for many reasons. One that is less often discussed is the mingling of finances. We've talked at length in this book about how marriage is a partnership, and that's as true for financial issues as it is for spiritual ones. Just as you might with spiritual challenges, you should communicate with your spouse and seek their counsel when matters dealing with money arise.

There are a few different things you can do to help ensure your marriage is strong, both emotionally and financially. We're going to take a look at some of the most important below.

Talk about money. How do you view money? You should talk about how you see money with your spouse. Are you on the same page about budgeting and saving for the future? This might not seem like a big discussion to have, but it's not uncommon for spouses to have different views of money. One might see things with an emphasis on the short-term. That means that they'll be more focused with what they need to spend money on right away rather than what they'll need in the future. This can also lead to spending money that should be saved because the individual in question simply doesn't take the future into account.

Other spouses might have an eye for the future. These individuals will understand the financial goals that both parties in the marriage are working to accomplish. This includes things like saving for a child or a home. They might not always be the most in tune with what the household needs on a daily basis, however, and could use some balancing out to compromise future financial goals with current needs.

If neither of you know how to save your money, don't panic! There are actually a number of different things you can do to help achieve financial literacy. You can take a course online, make an appointment with a financial planner, or seek the advice of individuals whom you know understand how to handle their money. Don't be shy about increasing your knowledge in this area. Many of us were not taught these skills and, like other skills, we have to learn and practice in order to be good at them. There is no shame in seeking to further your knowledge.

Talk about debts and assets. When you enter into marriage, you should do so honestly. That means that you shouldn't have secret debts or assets. Talk with your partner and be frank about money that you owe as well as money you might have hidden away in one form or another. Your assets, debt, and credit ratings are all factors that can influence how easy it is for you to find a home or start saving for the future, so it's vitally important that you don't keep information from each other.

Set goals and create a plan. Working together with your spouse, think about financial goals you'd like to accomplish. Discuss them and talk about why you think they're important. Once you understand why you're working towards a particular goal, sit down and create a budget with your spouse. This plan will help you create a roadmap of sorts from your current point to your goal. You can estimate the amount of time it should take you to achieve the goal, too, which helps strengthen the resolve to achieve it, while enabling you to plan around it. If you're saving for a home, for example, and are waiting to start a family until you have one, you might start to plan for your future family as you draw closer to your goal.

Talk about how to handle money. Is one of you going to be in charge of finances, or is that a task that is split between the two of you? Even if one of you will be responsible for paying bills and keeping track of savings accounts, make sure that you both have equal access to the accounts. You should never be in a position where you're wondering about your financial situation or just assuming that everything is fine. Your partner might handle the finances and pay the bills, but you should still know what you're bringing in and the progress that is being made towards your goal.

Throughout this book, we've talked about how important communication and loyalty is among spouses. All of that guidance holds true when it comes to finances.

Anthony and Carla. One of our couples, Anthony, 51, and Carla, 44, have been married for 19 years and felt that financial literacy was the most important advice they could give. They advise partners to "Communicate often and openly about financial responsibility and limitations."

You must be truthful with your spouse and speak respectfully about money. If one party spends more than is budgeted, that should be addressed as lovingly and frankly as possible. Try to remain calm and speak as objectively and kindly as possible. Always keep your financial goals in mind and discuss any issues that arise with your spouse as quickly as possible.

Chapter 6: Spirituality

DOES A STRONG, healthy, happy, and whole marriage have to have a spiritual base? Spirituality can be such a hot and polarizing topic. It evokes memories, good and bad, in many of us and some people prefer to steer clear of the subject all together. The goal of this chapter is not to convince/convert anyone toward any spiritual or religious preference; rather our goal is to continue to share common characteristics of the couples we've interviewed for this book. These are couples who have been married for 20 plus years, and their experiences are priceless.

There is an old southern saying, "Eat the meat and throw away the bone." This refers to using what you can from pieces of information and discarding the rest. The hope is that, even if you don't believe in spirituality or a single God, you may find nuggets of wisdom in this chapter that will provide a road map to a long, healthy, and successful marriage.

Hopefully, as you've moved progressively through this book, you have picked up a few tips that can enhance and compliment your marriage. Many aspects of marriage have been described in ways and with tools that can help in this wonderful journey with your spouse.

In order to keep a lasting bond, the couples we interviewed found it really helps both spouses to have a spiritual foundation. The importance of faith and a deep, unyielding relationship with God helps them get through the hardest and most confusing of times, as well as giving thanks to God for the times of bliss in your marriage – those times that are so good that you instinctively know they can only come from God.

In this chapter, we're going to take a closer look at faith and spirituality and take a peek at how spirituality has had an impact on marriage in the lives of the couples we interviewed for this book. All of them place a strong relationship with God as one of the most important factors in a long-lasting relationship.

Many experts in a variety of fields agree that spirituality is embedded in all aspects of life. In other words, all that we see, hear, touch, and breathe are oftentimes linked to our spiritual belief that our creator made all that we see, hear, smell, touch, and breathe. Spirituality is also the element we hold close to help us understand, or put in context, an occurrence in our lives that we simply can't explain. Whether it's enhancing something that's already good and making it better or taking a dark part of our lives and making it better, those of us, who have lived and been around the block a bit with this thing called life, understand this experience. For Christians, it's called God's Grace that stays with us in our best times, in our toughest times, and in all times throughout.

Frequently, the question is asked about the difference between spirituality and religion. Spirituality is often considered a vital part of religion and faith, which means that you might live a spiritual life while living a religious life, without even understanding the difference. Some say the difference is that religion asks the questions while spirituality guides the answers. Some may also say that religion gives you the rules to keep in mind as you move forward throughout your day.

For many, having faith (the evidence of things hoped for and the substance of things unseen) is a major part of ourselves and our marriage. This faith may have been instilled in us through our culture, through modeling and/or through our own concept of spirituality. So, the idea of giving up in a marriage is not an option for many couples who have a strong spiritual foundation.

Almost all couples interviewed for this book mentioned that a spiritual foundation as key to their marriage.

Howard and Erica. When sharing what most helped them throughout the years, Howard and Erica, married for 23 years, said that one of the most important stops they took along the way was "Learning biblical rules for their marriage." They had many bumps and bruises and their marriage was, once, on life-support as they experienced a dark stage where they almost filed for divorce in their 12th year.

Their advice? Don't be afraid to seek counseling. And make certain it's Christian counseling or marriage and family counseling by a therapist who is a Christian. As you can imagine, it helps tremendously when your counselor is a Christian, as well.

Howard and Erica went to counseling for one and a half years to get their marriage back on track. They went together and individually. The decision to seek counseling became such a positive experience that it taught them how to hold each other accountable to what the Bible says about marriage, as well as considering your spouse's feelings. They also learned that you must be connected to a bible teaching church, in order for a strong foundation to occur.

Howard and Erica mentioned that their church blessed their marriage in multiple ways. One being taught biblical roles. They also became active in their church and in Sunday school.

Robert and Sharon. Robert and Sharon are 50 years old and have been married 24 years. The following is a direct quote from this couple:

"An unshakable faith in God and each other is the key to our marriage. Faith in God demonstrates a submissive belief that our union is bigger than either one of us and collectively our destiny is part of God's larger design. Our children are a gift for Him, our home is a reflection of Him, and our lives (individually and collectively) are our honor and praise to Him. Faith in each other helps us to, one, weather the difficult times, and, two, respect the changes and growth that will occur in both of us, and remind us that our love is rooted in so much more than our physical attributes."

Gary and Tina Marie. The following quotes come directly from Gary and Tina, who have been married 23 years:

"Listen to each other and remember you're on the same team!"

"Be honest, flexible and open to change."

"Keep God first in your life . . . the couple that prays together, stays together."

Robert and Lenora. Both Robert and Lenora have a common strength of faith and are equally yoked. They've been married 20 years. They are both committed to their marriage.

"One thing that's constant in life is that things are bound to happen that can make life very tough and perhaps test your commitment to your marriage and your faith. Health, children, finances, LIFE, can all take a toll on a person and marriages. Having a firm spiritual foundation makes those tough times, smoother and bearable."

If you have not recently done so, sit down and have a conversation with your spouse about where you stand spiritually – both individually and together. How does spirituality manifest itself in your lives? Does it? How will it manifest in how you raise your children? Will it? Hopefully these questions can lead to deep meaningful conversations with one another. This will help you better understand each other and help you grow individually and together.

Chapter 7: Marital Roles

ONE ELEMENT THAT makes the experience of matrimony truly wonderful is knowing what your areas of responsibility are to keep the household productive and operational. It may sound like a business and, yes, from this perspective, business and marriage share similar commonalities.

Take Wal-Mart, for example. It's the largest retail employer in the country, running neck-and-neck with Amazon. Now, neither Amazon nor Wal-Mart would be able to run efficiently if everyone working for the company did not perform their assigned tasks and were not held accountable. From the cashier to the customers, everyone has a role and one is just important as the other. This is true in general society, as well.

There are millions of people living in the U.S. Collectively, we all make up a society. Societies function smoothly when everyone works together, even when one does not realize they are doing so.

A household is the same way. Each spouse, and even the children, have roles and responsibilities that are oftentimes based on traditions and strengths to keep that household running smoothly. The key to successfully assigning these responsibilities is via a strong marriage.

Both parties in a marriage need to know they have roles that will contribute to the success of the marriage. Maslow's Hierarchy of Needs is a psychological theory depicted as a five-tiered pyramid of human needs. Sitting at the top of the pyramid, which represents the highest need for a human, is self-actualization. That means that it's important to develop a purpose for life. The same can be said for marriages. The highest, most well-functioning form of a marriage is when the marriage has a purpose. Roles can help develop that purpose.

What Roles Exist in a Healthy Marriage?

The truth is that it can be difficult to define roles that perfectly fit every marriage because every relationship is unique. The dynamic that works for one couple might not work well for you and your partner, at all.

There are a few different ways of looking at marital roles, however, that can help answer the next question.

What do you already do? It is fairly rare to find a relationship where no roles have organically developed. That's because relationships take a lot of time and effort. The ones that last and make it to marriage are, hopefully, those in which the couple is dedicated to helping each other and building a life together. To help accomplish this task, each individual begins to sacrifice a bit for the sake of the other.

Perhaps one partner cooks dinner every night because the other works late, for example, but the partner that works late swings by the store on their way home since they're already out. Perhaps neither individual is thrilled about those activities, but they settle into them quickly because the health of the relationship itself often depends on them.

Take a look at your own relationship. Is there something that you do consistently? This can be anything. Maybe you always do the dishes, for example, or know when to start a pot of tea for your spouse. Perhaps they do the same for you. These are roles that are not always verbally defined, but that makes them no less important. In fact, these roles evolve, in large part, because they are vital to making the relationship work.

Talk to your partner and discuss what you see. Do they agree with your perception of the existing roles in your relationship? Are they happy with them?

Take some time over pizza or a mindless reality show to do this. Make it fun! List all of the responsibilities you both see as necessary in order to maintain a smooth-running household. You will want to identify those responsibilities – the ones that, if they were not done, would immediately cause issues. Not doing them isn't conducive to an orderly, healthy, and romance-promoting environment.

What more needs to be done? You might think that, since you already have certain roles established in your relationship, you don't need to search for anything more. That is not the case. In fact, as your relationship evolves, you are likely to find there are adjustments to be made and new roles to undertake. If you're wondering how to do this, you already know the answer. Talk to your partner.

Communication is absolutely vital in healthy relationships, and that's especially true about something as important as marital/relationship roles. Failing to talk openly about these things can lead to resentment and anger. Perhaps you're completely satisfied with the division of housework, for example, or with who does the cooking or handles the children at night. But is your spouse? Maybe they'd like to spend more time with your children – or, conversely, maybe they're exhausted after long shifts at work and could use some down time instead of the chaos that sometimes reigns with children at night.

Try taking some time to list all the responsibilities you see in your relationship. These are things that, if they weren't done, would throw the house or relationship itself into chaos. Things like housework are important, of course, but also go a bit deeper. Think about what you need from your spouse on an emotional level, too, in order to thrive. Be honest about those feelings and be direct about what you'd like to see. Encourage your partner to do the same.

Most people will advocate a relationship in which both parties work towards a common goal – the life they want to live. They do this by supporting each other and running a functional household and family. Respect and love are absolutely vital to building a healthy relationship and the only way you can achieve that is by being honest and frank with each other.

Be flexible. One important note I'd like to make here is that roles are not set in stone. What works for your relationship at one point might not work after a few years. This is especially true when you factor in things like health issues, job changes, and children to the mix. It's quite likely that you'll need to revisit these roles and, sometimes, pick up each other's slack.

And that's okay. No one is perfect and having a set role in a relationship doesn't mean that if the person who usually upholds the responsibilities inherent to that role fails to do so, the work just doesn't get done. Take house chores, for example. Maybe you have more free time than your spouse, or simply work fewer hours, and so you do a bit more of the housework than they do. If you fall ill and are unable to complete those chores, should your spouse just shrug their shoulders and let things pile up?

Of course not. You each take on certain roles to maintain a healthy and functional household. If one of you is unable to do what you normally do, then the other partner steps in and does it instead. You are, after all, *partners*. You're in this relationship together and are working together to create a loving and happy home. Don't get stuck in the mindset of "well, if they don't do the dishes, I guess they just don't get done this week." Step in and help your partner and expect them to step in and help you, too.

You both have to be flexible. Acknowledge that life is often a winding path and you might very well end up taking a few unexpected turns that lead you to unforeseen destinations. Be kind to each other during these road stops. Help each other and do what needs to be done to keep your relationship running smoothly.

How are Marriage Roles Maintained in a Healthy Marriage?

The question about how to establish and maintain roles in a marriage is a common one. You might find yourself wondering how to, exactly, navigate this topic with your significant other. In reality, this doesn't need to be a difficult conversation. As we've already outlined, marriage roles are born from love and respect – and there's no shame in loving and supporting your partner just as there's no shame in sacrificing to make them happy.

Marriage roles look like a well-oiled machine in healthy relationships. They're something that both partners actively uphold, but not roles they necessarily have to consciously assume. For many people, especially after years of marriage, it becomes second nature to support your spouse in order to create a cohesive whole. It might even feel intuitive. If you've been around couples who have been married for a long time, you might have seen this in action. One spouse might say or do something and the other immediately steps in to support them – not obtrusively, but subtly and matter-of-factly.

These roles are established and maintained through clear communication. What do you need from your spouse in order to thrive? Be honest with your partner. Talk about what makes you feel supported and loved, and how your partner can help. Ask them the same questions. Marriage requires effort from both partners – it is a *partnership,* after all.

Don't be afraid to have clear and frank conversations about this, especially if circumstances change and you need something different out of the relationship. Dynamics change, but they don't have to break a relationship. It's possible to grow together and continue to love and support each other for decades.

Marital Roles in Long-Term, Committed Relationships

In order to best understand what marital roles look like in long-term, committed relationships, let's take a look at what some of the couples we've interviewed had to say about the subject.

Howard and Erica. Howard and Erica, married for 23 years, recognize the importance of learning about roles and sticking to them to help manage their marriage:

"One, learning biblical rules for the marriage. We had many bumps and bruises and have even been on life-support. It wasn't until we hit a dark stage for marriage in years 12 and 13 that we almost got divorced. Don't be afraid to seek counseling. For us, it had to be Christian counseling. We went to counseling for one and a half years to get back on track. We went together and individually. This held us accountable to what the Word (Bible) says about our marriage and not own feelings and beliefs. Two, we must be connected to a Bible teaching church. It was a connection with the church that allowed us to be around other believers that held us accountable. Here's how our church has blessed our marriage: It helped Erica have a safe place to reach out to her Sunday school teachers when I was acting a fool. Years later, we have become the lead teachers of the same class. Learning my biblical role as a husband led me through a man's disciple process."

Thomas and Lisa. Thomas and Lisa, married 25 years, agree that clear roles are vital to the health of their marriage. They also believe that being flexible and caring in those roles is important:

"Role clarification is important for us. We found out early in our marriage that, without communicating about roles, we assumed each of us were going to do things that never occurred. This led to several headaches: no food cooked, bills not paid, etc. We quickly fell into traditional roles in our marriage. Lisa cooked and Thomas took care of the yard, cars, and bills. After a few years, we realized that neither one of us wanted to be solely responsible for those items. We discussed how to divide them up and we communicated what felt good and what didn't. We each still have a primary responsibility for those roles but it's not so rigid that if Lisa is working late, we all sit in the house with hunger pains until she comes home or if I'm traveling for 10 days that I come home to grass 10 inches tall. We are able to flow between our roles in order to keep the household functioning nicely."

Alan and Mickey. Alan and Mickey, married for over 26 years, keep it short and simple when it comes to their thoughts about marital roles. They believe open communication and respect is the most important factor to keep in mind:

"One of the many things that have kept us together and happy for 26 plus years is we communicate but stay in our lanes when it comes to our children and grandchildren. We don't step on each other's toes. That's a definite no-no!"

Understanding the importance of marital roles is vital in a marriage. The roles that and your spouse develop are YOURS and do not have to look like others in your extended family, neighborhood, church, etc. Mary Kay and Walmart may function very differently in terms of operations, yet they are both successful. Communication, trust, transparency, and flexibility are characteristics that are needed to have healthy and productive conversations with your spouse around roles. Once you identified them, they can help your marriage find its purpose and you'll soon be living the best marital life possible.

Chapter 8: The Myth of 50/50

WE'VE COME A long way. From looking at the meaning of love to thinking about what roles spirituality and loyalty play in a strong marriage, we've covered quite a bit of territory in this book. We hope you have found tips and tools that can help you keep a vibrant and happy marriage.

As we reach the final chapter, you might be tempted to tune out a bit – after all, you've already read so much, and the end is near! But please . . . stay in there and stay focused. This chapter happens to be one of the most important.

As you build strong relationships and begin to fall into a groove of give and take, you might wonder exactly how much you should "give" and how much to "take." These are worthy questions! You don't want to give until you're ragged, after all, because that's not fair to anyone. If you've given everything you have nothing left for yourself. It's also not okay to take and take and take with no regard to your spouse's needs and run the risk of them giving until they break.

Marriage is all about compromise, respect, and love. These aren't new concepts, of course, and we've explored them all quite thoroughly in other chapters. You have probably heard somewhere that marriage should be a 50/50 compromise (cue Teddy Pendergrass). We want to take some time to tell you why we think the concept of marriage being 50/50 is a myth and how you might consider approaching your marriage from a healthier place.

What is the "Myth of 50/50?"

When people talk about marriage, they often emphasize that it's a collaborative process. And that's true – marriage is very much something that both parties involved undertake together. It doesn't work if only one person is putting in effort. The work must be balanced in some way so that both spouses are both giving and receiving enough from their relationship. Because we like to be fair it makes sense that the work in question is often said to be a "50/50 split" in a marriage.

In theory, the concept is a good one. When everything is split down the middle, both partners are giving just as much as the other. It probably even seems like dividing things up in this way would ensure that everyone involved feels like they're doing as much as they should and that it might actually help avoid arguments. The problem is that, in practice, that's not what happens with a 50/50 mentality.

When you put a definitive percentage on how much effort you're going to put into a marriage, you naturally begin to keep tabs of your actions as well as your spouse's. You might notice that you've done a bit more than they have, for example, especially when it comes to things like housework or childcare. That perceived inequality can quickly turn to resentment if left to fester for too long. You might start to dwell on the idea that you're putting in "too much" effort and feel like there's a point where you shouldn't have to try anymore. But when it comes to healthy marriages, that's not really a point you should experience.

Another reason why "50/50" is a myth is that it gives the idea that each spouse only gives 50% of their effort. That is the wrong idea to have. Strong marriages are marriages where both spouses are 100% committed to making the relationship work. They continually build each other up and focus on ensuring that they are moving forward each day. That means each is giving 100% of their effort to their spouse, to their marriage, and to their family.

Have you ever provided 50% effort to anything that you really prioritized? Be it a job search, looking for a partner, trying to lose weight . . . anything? If you put 50% effort toward achieving that goal you probably didn't achieve it. You cannot have a healthy, happy marriage if both spouses are only willing to give 50% of their effort – that's just now how relationships work. Or, to be a bit more specific, that's not how *healthy* relationships work. Healthy relationships require a lot of work. There is an immense amount of give and take that occurs, and the truth is that this can look different for every couple. In general, however, it might help to look at marriage as a "100/100" split instead of a "50/50." You're both giving your all, in order to create the best marriage possible.

But what exactly does this split look like in real life? Let's take a look.

What Does a Healthy Division of Effort and Work Look Like in a Committed and Long-Term Relationship?

First and foremost, you must be invested in your relationship in order to put in the work required to build a committed and long-term marriage. With that in mind, the division of labor and effort can look wildly different from couple to couple. Dr. Melanie Joell, a Washington D.C. based therapist, put it best – each couple dances their own dance. Some relationships might have one spouse working outside the home while the other takes care of keeping the home running smoothly. Others will see both spouses working outside of the home and working together to ensure they are equally happy.

One thing that doesn't change, however, is the way that spouses, who have a healthy division of effort and work, interact with each other. They communicate openly and often, for example, and keep each other updated about their challenges and their struggles, as well as their victories. This is important, because the way that life is going outside the home can affect how you're behaving inside it. If you're having a particularly rough patch at work, for example, and find yourself worried about a particular situation, you might find that you struggle more to take on the same number of chores you might have taken on in the past.

In a healthy relationship, both spouses can sit down and recognize that there is a temporary issue that's impacting the balance of give and take a bit. You can adjust for that change, then, by realizing that your spouse is doing their best and could really use some extra support. You might be shouldering more than you're comfortable with for a bit, but you should be reassured that if the roles were reversed and you needed that extra help, your spouse would do the same.

Communicate (there's that word, again) openly and often with each other in a supportive and effective way around effort. Keep each other updated with the challenges and struggles you may face, on a daily basis, and remember to celebrate each other's victories, both large and small!

Here are some guidelines to help you better recognize what a healthy split of effort and work looks like in a committed marriage.

You're equally exhausted. I know, this might not sound like the best way to determine success in a marriage. If you're both exhausted, after all, are things really going that well?

To put it bluntly, yes. It is entirely possible for both spouses in a healthy marriage to be utterly exhausted at the same time. Life is hard and building a long-term marriage that lasts can be hard as well. You might find that keeping the relationship going requires every ounce of effort both of you can pour into it. And that's okay. The important thing is that you're working together to build a healthy and happy connection that withstands challenges.

If you're both equally exhausted, then you're both giving as much effort as you can to the marriage. This also includes building a family and a happy home. If one spouse works outside the home and returns after an incredibly difficult day to find the other spouse chipper and full of energy thanks to a relaxing day spent lounging about all day, there might be an issue with the division of effort and work in that relationship.

If one spouse comes home tired and finds their spouse equally tired after a day spent running errands, corralling children, and keeping appointments at church or with family, you can see that the effort is much more evenly given.

This might also mean that neither of you are exhausted – that's the dream, right? A happy and fulfilling marriage doesn't have to be a challenge, especially not after you've established your careers and understand the role you play in the relationship. And, of course, this is just one small, over-simplified guideline to keep in mind. Maybe your relationship is different. If it works for both of you, then that's great. Remember, each couple dances their own dance.

You help each other. In addition to being equally exhausted as a result of expending 100% of your energy and effort on the relationship, a healthy marriage will see both spouses helping each other wherever possible. That means that if you see your wife is struggling after a long day and you can afford to jump in and help make her life easier, you do so without being asked. You should both be asking yourselves what you can do to help make your spouse's life easier.

As you move through your day, keep an eye on how you're feeling and how your spouse is feeling. Listen to what they're telling you. Could they use help with something, even if they're not explicitly asking for your aid or expecting you to provide it? Then give some effort and work alongside them. Marriage isn't about declaring a "winner" between the two of you. You are a team, after all! It's about working in tandem to create a happy and healthy relationship based on respect, observance, loyalty, and love.

If you do end up helping out a bit more than you might otherwise, don't keep tabs on that effort. If you're only helping with the intention of calling in a "favor" at a later date, it might be time to reevaluate your priorities. That's not how you build a loving marriage. That's how you end up in divorce court. Instead, give without the expectation of receiving. You're working hard because you want your spouse to be happy and when your spouse is happy, you are happy. When you are both happy your relationship is strong, and you are both thriving individually and as a team.

You're not afraid to ask for help. One big issue with the 50/50 mindset is that when one spouse needs some extra support or help, they find themselves afraid to ask for it because their spouse has already "given their 50%" that week or that day. They feel as though it's unfair to ask for more since they personally aren't able to give more of themselves at that time.

In a healthy marriage, you shouldn't be scared to ask for support. You and your spouse are both committed to being together forever, right? So, supporting each other is just another part of building a strong relationship. This is another area where the idea of "give and take" comes into play. Maybe you need to take a little bit more today, but you might very well end up giving a bit more tomorrow. Marriage has a way of balancing these efforts.

If you find that you *are* afraid to ask for help, it might be time to sit down and really think about why that is. Talk to your spouse openly and explain what you're feeling and why you feel that way. You can't support each other 100% if you're not being completely honest with each other, so don't hesitate to discuss even difficult topics. Remember that marriage is about loving respect, not carefully tracking each and every effort you make for each other. Keeping tabs is a no-no! If you are doing that, stop it!

The bottom line is that marriage is a collaborative effort and should be seen as such. You're not each giving 50% of a whole – you're giving 100% to create a strong, unbreakable foundation upon which you'll build your lives. So be kind to your spouse and be understanding when things don't go the way you thought they might. You'll walk many winding paths together over the course of a long-term and committed marriage.

What do our couples have to say about the division of effort and work in a healthy and happy relationship? Let's take a look.

Thomas and Lisa. Over our many years together, they realized that the idea of 50/50 simply isn't realistic. Here's how they came to that conclusion.

After about 18 months into the marriage, Thomas began to count up all of the things that he had given up in order to make the marriage work. All day college football on Saturday, all day NFL on Sunday, time at the gun range three times a week, and happy hour three times a week. He began to keep tabs and notice when Lisa was getting was getting her hair done, her nails done, etc. In a fit of frustration, he listed all the things he had given up for the marriage. Guess what? Lisa listed all the things she had given up, and her list was longer than his!

They realized then what they already knew: keeping tabs on who's giving more in the relationship is a no-win game. "We both give our all to our marriage because it is the highest priority for us."

Anthony and Carla. Anthony and Carla also had a few things to say about the idea of a strictly 50/50 marriage.

"50/50 is a joke. Life doesn't work that way. It ebbs and flows, and you have to roll with it. It's like a game of Spades. Sometimes you'll have three books and your partner will have four books and you'll win a hand. Sometimes you'll have six and your partner will have one and you'll win the hand. In both cases the input is not the same, yet you win the hand because in both cases each gives all they have."

Collaborative effort in a 100/100 marriage. Our couples understand the importance of open and honest support without the expectation of accolades. In fact, many of them credit their ability to support and love each other even when times are difficult as one of the most important aspects of a healthy marriage.

Thomas Adams

Conclusion

AND THERE YOU have it -- tips about marriage and how to make it work. We believe the tips shared are tried and true and remain constant across demographics.

We started this book with the intention of writing a book to celebration African American / Black marriage.

When you think about it, as other cultures are in their own right, African Americans are a unique culture that comes with peculiar challenges given the history of African Americans in the U.S.

Some of us come from homes that were dysfunctional, with dads who left and never came back or were in and out of our lives. Some of us had one or both parents with some type of substance abuse habit or experienced extreme poverty and the impact of racism, etc. Whatever the challenge is or was, some of us do not know what it means to be successful and loyal at being a spouse because it was not modeled in our lives as we were growing up. It just wasn't something we saw when we were young. Yet many of us have found ways to flourish. Our goal with this book was to document the ways in which the African American couples we interviewed flourished and to point out best practices of a good marriage.

It should go without saying that some of the challenges mentioned above are not exclusive to African Americans. What we are suggesting is that African Americans are a unique culture and with the constant narrative that Black marriages are a myth, it's important to have a book on strong Black marriages that have lasted the test of time.

A strong, healthy marriage takes work! It's not something that just magically happens overnight. If anything, we hope this book has reinforced the notion that, along with the value of putting in the time and hard work, marriage takes persistence and determination. Your marriage probably requires the most time of any activity or relationship in which you've been involved. However, the rewards are incredible and there are benefits in our communities as well. In addition to love and happiness, marriage comes with benefits.

Financial Benefits

There are financial benefits that we don't talk about or educate ourselves about enough in our communities. We won't say marriage is a business, however, what we will say is that marriage consists of concepts of business that are required for both spouses to agree upon in order to find success. A few financial benefits[1] of marriage include:

Tax Benefits

- Filing joint income tax returns with the IRS and state taxing authorities.

- Creating a "family partnership" under federal tax laws, which allows you to divide business income among family members.

Estate Planning Benefits

- Inheriting a share of your spouse's estate.

- Receiving an exemption from both estate taxes and gift taxes for all property you give or leave to your spouse.

- Creating life estate trusts that are restricted to married couples, including QTIP trusts, QDOT trusts, and marital deduction trusts.

---

[1] From https://www.nolo.com/legal-encyclopedia/marriage-rights-benefits-30190.html

- Obtaining priority if your spouse needs a conservator--that is, someone to make financial or medical decisions on your spouse's behalf.

Government Benefits

- Receiving Social Security, Medicare, and disability benefits for spouses.

- Receiving veterans' and military benefits for spouses, such as those for education, medical care, or special loans.

- Receiving public assistance benefits.

Employment Benefits

- Obtaining insurance benefits through a spouse's employer.

- Taking family leave to care for your spouse during an illness.

- Receiving wages, workers' compensation, and retirement plan benefits for a deceased spouse.

- Taking bereavement leave if your spouse or one of your spouse's close relatives dies.

Medical Benefits

- Visiting your spouse in a hospital intensive care unit or during restricted visiting hours in other parts of a medical facility.

- Making medical decisions if your spouse becomes incapacitated and unable to express wishes for treatment.

Death Benefits

- Consenting to after-death examinations and procedures.

- Making burial or other final arrangements.

Family Benefits

- Filing for stepparent or joint adoption.

- Applying for joint foster care rights.

- Receiving a share of marital property if you divorce.

- Receiving spousal or child support, child custody, and visitation if you divorce.

Housing Benefits

- Living in neighborhoods zoned for "families only."

- Automatically renewing leases signed by your spouse.

Consumer Benefits

- Receiving family rates for health, homeowners, auto, and other types of insurance.

- Receiving tuition discounts and permission to use school facilities.

- Other consumer discounts and incentives available only to married couples or families.

A strong, healthy marriage takes work! We hope that is book provides real life practical tools and concepts to help you develop and strong and healthy marriage. Getting married was the best decision in our lives and deciding to work at our marriage has enriched both of our lives immensely.

Afterthought

THROUGHOUT THIS BOOK we've spent a lot of time, what we like to call "quality-time," talking about relationships, marriage, love, loyalty, and trust. We also offered a bit of what amounts to self-improvement. We encourage you to refer to this book as something more than "just a book about marriage." We hope you remember and refer to it as a valuable tool that helped you check out your marriage via a different, cleaner and clearer lens that encourages you to fight through the toughest times and acknowledge/celebrate the smallest victories.

Marriage also has other benefits that it brings to our communities, such as teaching and training on patient, committed, loyal, and accountable households. You see, as we stated earlier, marriage brings structure and accountability that many of us need in our lives to really be productive and focused. Marriage brings out the best and worst in us. Those that make it through the difficult times and ride the waves of life with their spouse, under any condition that's not toxic and unsafe, who acknowledges and celebrates the smallest victories, provides and encourages support, respects each other and accepts the spouse for who they are, are on the right track to reaping all the privileges and benefits of marriage.

Whether you're just beginning your journey or are hoping for some guidance to find your way back to the right path, we hope the information and advice in this book can serve as a sort of guide for you and your spouse to find your way through a rough patch to smooth ground.

You'll notice that in this book we speak from a 'we' perspective. That's intentional. We are separate individuals AND a joined unit. We approach things through a united front so our response to the topics in this book are on one accord.

Now, as we close, we want to share with you what starts it all! No matter how shy, introverted, confused or in disbelief you may be early on in a relationship that results in marriage, please remember that your actions speak loudly, but your eyes speak even louder and clearer! Let the lyrics of the song, "This Love is Forever," resonate a bit:

"You don't have to say this love's forever

I can see it in your eyes tonight

You don't have talk about tomorrow

hold me in your arms tonight

My love

"Silently you and me

caress each other's hearts desperately

We long to be lover's forever

"Wanting you the way I do

burns a fire deep inside

touching you I never knew I could feel this way

"You don't have to say this love is forever

I can see it in your eyes tonight

you don't have to talk about tomorrow

hold me in your arms tonight my love

"So, tonight will love

inside a warmth comes over me

Passion high

feel so right

love eternity

"Words cannot begin to tell the way I feel for you

we share a special kind of love that's only shared by two

Words cannot begin to tell the way you make me feel

Unspoken is our passion; we share a love that's real...

Love!"

God Bless.

References

Cowan, C. and Kaniel, N. (1994). This Love is Forever [Recorded by H. Hewett]. On *It's Time* [CD]. UK. Expansion Records.

Joell, Dr. M.L. (n.d.). Loving Connections Psychotherapy, LLC. *Psychology Today*. Retrieved from https://www.psychologytoday.com/us/therapists/loving-connections-psychotherapy-llc-oxon-hill-md/287001

Nolo.com (n.d.). Marriage Rights and Benefits. Retrieved from https://www.nolo.com/legal-encyclopedia/marriage-rights-benefits-30190.html

Thomas Adams

About the Authors

THOMAS AND LISA SAYLES-ADAMS have been happily married for over 25 years. They have four adult children and a grandson. They have been through just about everything a couple can go through: Trust challenges, blended family, financial difficulties, learning to grow together, etc. Throughout all the challenges a young couple could face, Thomas and Lisa have managed to remain a loving and connected family for over two decades. Thomas is a strong advocate of family and believes in highlighting the beauty he sees every day: African American families thriving. He is the President and CEO of a leading nonprofit organization in Minneapolis, MN. He graduated with an undergraduate degree from North Dakota State University, a master's from Augsburg College, and earned his PhD from Regent University. He's a sought-after speaker on criminal justice reform, nonprofit management, and leadership, among other topics. Lisa is an accomplished educator with over 25 years of experience. She's currently an Associate Superintendent in a midwestern urban school district. She graduated with a Political Science degree from the University of Minnesota and a Master's in Education from St. Kate's University. She's currently completing her Ed.D at Minnesota State Mankato. She's a frequent consultant on curriculum and design, middle school reform, and parent engagement. Besides their children, what they are most proud of is the 25+ couples they have mentored over the years.

Made in the USA
Monee, IL
10 November 2020